To the memory of my mother, Julia, who gave me breath and taught me to draw it deeply before any journey.

—P.M.

Published by Yeehoo Press
6540 Lusk Blvd, Ste C152, San Diego, CA 92121
yeehoopress.com

The illustrations for this book were painted with acrylic gouache and edited in Photoshop .
Edited by Yao Shen
Designed by Chao Zhang
Supervised by Luyang Xue

Library of Congress Control Number: 2023930711
ISBN:978-1-953458-62-9
Printed in China First Edition
1 2 3 4 5 6 7 8 9 10

My Breathing Earth

Written by Paul Many

Illustrated by Tisha Lee

YEEHOO
PRESS

Earth's breath slips through my
window each morning,
welcoming me to a new day.

It flutters my eyelashes
and brushes soft fingers
across my cheeks.

"Rise and shine, sweet girl of mine,"

I hear Mommy say.

Full of the smell of rain
that tapped on our roof all night,
Earth's breath
balloons our curtains.

As we sail from the bedroom,
the air musses the hair
of my little sister
and wiggles Buddy's ears
as he watches over her.

Indigo lifts her
head to see where
we are going so early.
She will sleep the whole
day long, breezes ruffling
her fur.

Downstairs, the air turns
the corners of Daddy's newspaper
and wrinkles the top of the tea
in Mommy's cup.

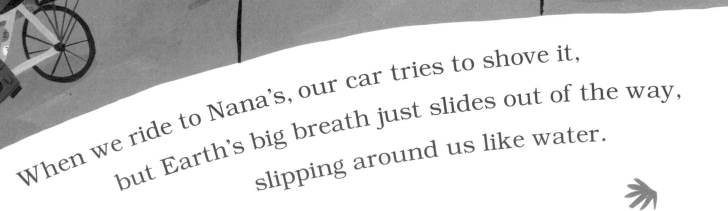

When we ride to Nana's, our car tries to shove it,
but Earth's big breath just slides out of the way,
slipping around us like water.

It plays with people in the street,
twirling their clothes into ice-cream swirls,
pushing them along to help them
get where they're going.

It waves Nana's bright flag as Mommy and Daddy drive away to work, scooping up leaves and scribbling them in a whirl behind their car.

We can't see Earth's breath,
but the arrow on Nana's garage
tells us where it's coming from.
And we can hear it tinkle the glass birds
hanging on her wind chime.

Puffing the tiny parachutes
of dandelion seeds far and wide,
it whirls whirlybirds
off the big maple tree.

It dances the little suns
of pie pans hanging
around her vegetable garden,

scaring the squirrels so they don't dig her carrots.

Earth's breath bounces our bubbles like little boats bobbing.

It glides our paper planes like the ones that fly—so tiny!— high in the sky.

It ripples the walls of sheets
as we play hide-and-seek
between them.

And calms the friends
that Nana has over this morning.
They sit quietly in her living room
and let it flow in and out of them.

She lets us sit with her
if we stay quiet too.

Even though it's mostly kind,

Earth's breath sometimes plays tricks,
slamming Nana's screen door
or tipping her plants off the porch railing.

But then it seems sorry,

sweeping away all the mess it made.

It rises up under our kites,
bouncing them up and down the way
Daddy bounces me when he
and Mommy come to bring us home.

As I wash my hands and face, it carries the smells of dinner up to me.

At bedtime it rushes about,
busily pulling dark smudges
of clouds aside, so the smiling moon
can light my room.

It rustles my curtains,
parting them to the million stars
spinning about our house.

In dreams, I feel Earth's breath rise and fall under me, like I'm lying on the stomach of something big and warm and soft.

Rolling and rolling, Earth turns like a Ferris wheel as I sleep, slowly moving until the morning sun starts to peek through my open window.

"Rise and shine, sweet girl of mine,"
I hear Mommy say, waking me
as Earth's fresh breath
drifts over me again,

welcoming me to another day.

Our Breathing Earth

Earth's breath slips in our windows in the morning and surrounds us all day. Most people simply call it "air." But I wanted to show it as a part of a living Earth, one that has a "breath" like all of us.

As our Earth spins and is heated by the sun, its breath blows flags and laundry, sails boats, and flies kites. We may feel it as everything from gentle breezes, to gusts and gales, and sometimes even hurricanes and tornadoes!

We also breathe the Earth's breath: gently when resting and more sharply when running and playing. As we do, it fills us with something called oxygen, which our bodies need.

The Earth's breath also forms a kind of shell, protecting our planet from some harmful rays of the sun as well as those from faraway exploding stars. It shields us from pieces of rock flying through space.

But lately, it has become more and more dirty because of pollution from things like factories and cars. This pollution causes the air to act like a lid. The sun heats the Earth, and much of the warmth that radiates from the Earth is trapped.

Earth gets hotter. The sea rises as water from melted ice runs into it. Cities that are near the oceans have more floods, and storms get stronger, causing more damage. Some places get very dry, making it hard to grow food.

What can we do?

We can help our Earth breathe better and stay cooler by walking and bicycling instead of riding in cars, and by doing such things as growing plants, which help keep the air clean.

We can share our Earth's breath with others by sitting quietly and paying attention as it flows in and out of us.